Profitable Newsletters

*The Step-by-Step Guide
to Attracting Eager-to-Buy Clients
With Your Email Newsletter*

by

Tammi Metzler

DISCLAIMER:
While the author has strived to provide accurate, complete information as of the date of publication, she cannot guarantee that the contents within are accurate at the time of reading due to the rapidly-changing nature of the Internet.

Furthermore, the information presented herein represents the view of the author as of the date of publication. Due to the rate at which conditions change, the author reserves the right to alter and update her opinion based on the new conditions. This book is for informational purposes only. While every attempt has been made to verify the information provided in this book, neither the author nor her affiliates/partners assume any responsibility for errors, inaccuracies or omissions. Any perceived slights of specific organizations or people, whether living or dead, are unintentional. This book is not intended for use as a source of legal, business, or financial advice. If advice concerning legal or related matters is needed, please seek the services of a fully qualified professional.

This book can offer no guarantees of income made. Readers are advised to rely on their own judgment about their individual circumstances and act accordingly.

Readers should be aware of any laws that govern business transactions or other business practices in their country and state before conducting business.

This book is lovingly dedicated to my supportive husband and beautiful daughter, both of whom very patiently picked up the slack at home while I was hard at work on this book. I would like to extend a heartfelt thank you to my parents and in-laws, who offered their undying support in so many ways. I love you guys. I want to also thank my eagle-eyes editor, Rachael Sefren, and tirelessly patient cover designer, Kate Rice, for their unfailing dedication to making this book the best it can be.

Table of Contents

Profitable Newsletters

Introduction

It seemed to happen all at once. I'd been forcing myself to publish my e-newsletter on a regular basis – twice a month, every month – despite a distinct – and noticeable – lack of responses from people on my newsletter list. I wasn't sure if they were even reading my messages, or if all that hard work was being wasted. Sure, here and there I'd get an inquiry into my services right after my e-newsletter was published, but other than that, all was quiet on the newsletter front.

Then, one day – out of the blue, it seemed – I noticed that people were treating me differently. I was getting emails from people who'd been on my newsletter list for 6 months, a year, more and more often. They were asking for advice, for my professional opinion. They were offering their services to me. They wanted to hire me to help them. They considered me a – gasp – expert in copywriting and marketing.

Why? Because I'd been feeding them useful marketing tips and helpful information. Every two weeks, I sent them something new, such as a few nuggets on writing better website copy or techniques to get started with article marketing. Whenever I came across new information, I eagerly shared it with them. Anything that would help them grow their businesses, I wanted them to have.

It wasn't always revolutionary information, either; some of the things that seemed like second nature to me, because I'd been doing it so long, were brand new to those who *weren't* studying marketing all day, every day. In fact, some of the newsletter issues that I thought were old news received the greatest responses and rave reviews from readers. Who knew?

The moral of the story is that everyone has something useful to share, and the purpose of this book is to show you how to get that information out of your head and into the creation of a powerful marketing funnel that will help you authentically draw your ideal clients toward your products and services.

If that sounds good to you, let's get started already!

Chapter 1: So, What's A Marketing Funnel?

If you haven't yet heard of the marketing funnel concept, the idea is that you can draw prospects to you with a free gift and then gradually introduce them to a low-price paid product, such as an e-book, followed by a more expensive program, like a home study course or group coaching program, followed by your most expensive – and therefore most valuable – offering, which is typically one-on-one services from you.

A solid marketing funnel that draws hot prospects to you and allows you to stay in touch with them does four very important things to help you build a strong business:

1. Build the know, like, and trust factor
2. Establish your expertise

3. Diversify your business

4. Let people "test" your services with little to no commitment

Let's explore each of those concepts in more detail, shall we?

Build the know, like, and trust factor

If you want to build a community of prospects that will buy your products and services, your first priority should be in attracting your prospects to your community, and then doing everything you can to build the know, like, and trust factor.

Here's the know, like, and trust factor in a nutshell:

KNOW – Getting people to **know** that you're there, ready to help them. Sounds way too simple, I know – that's because it is! In a nutshell, the "know" factor is all about putting yourself out there so that people will at the very least know that you're there to help them.

LIKE - The next step is getting people to **like** you. This doesn't mean false flattery or anything insincere; it's as simple as being yourself (you'll naturally attract your ideal clients this way) and being truly respectful of potential clients. That includes responding courteously to their inquiries, in addition to offering helpful advice and suggestions in things like your blog posts and email newsletters.

TRUST - **Trust** is built by the little things you do and say on a regular basis. For example, send out your email newsletter when you say you will; if you promise a publishing schedule of the 2nd & 4th Thursday of every month, even just sticking to that schedule will go a long way towards building the trust factor. Ditto with offering quality content in your blog posts, newsletters, teleseminars, etc.; keep feeding great stuff to your community, and they will soon begin to trust that you're the expert you claim to be.

As mentioned on the previous page, first you spread the word about yourself to get people into your community, then you let the real you shine through so they learn to love you (what's not to love, after all?) – and don't forget to share the love by responding to any concerns or inquiries promptly and courteously, and then bombard them with quality information so they trust that you know what you're talking about and can truly help them solve their problems.

I can't tell you how many times people have come to me after being on my newsletter for 6 months, 10 months, or longer, and said that they appreciated my quality content sent religiously every other Tuesday and trusted me as the one person who could help them get the results they wanted in their business. It's a great feeling to have such a win-win situation – I get a new client, and they get the help they need to grow their businesses.

Establish your expertise

Also, as I touched on previously, having a solid marketing funnel in place can do wonders for your expert status. Many of the "gurus" out there didn't wait for someone to come and hand them an award or certifications that qualified them as an expert in their field – actually, they didn't wait for anyone else to call them an expert at all...they just claimed the title for themselves.

Of course, it goes without saying that if you don't know the first thing about horse training, it's not a good idea to run around proclaiming yourself a horse training expert. As soon as you open your mouth, people will know that you're clueless on the subject. If, however, you've been an accounting assistant for 10 years and are now looking to branch out on your own as a virtual bookkeeping assistant to small business owners, it's a safe bet to say that you know a lot more about even basic accounting principles than most of your prospective clients. And if you know how to use specialized software to make their lives 10 times easier, save them bundles of time that they'd otherwise waste trying to muddle through their own finances, AND alert them to deductions and other cash-saving goodies...you've got a client for life, my friend.

Don't ever undervalue your own knowledge. A topic that may seem like second nature to you – way too basic to be worth anything – could quite literally spark an "a-ha!" moment that saves your target market time, helps them grow their business, earns them more money, etc. Once they see you providing all of this consistent, expert

Profitable Newsletters

advice, their shift to regarding you as THE expert in your field will follow automatically.

Diversify your business

Growing your business depends upon diversifying what you have to offer. If all you provide is high-cost service packages (even service packages that are on the low end pricewise could be well out of the budget for prospects), you're going to be severely limited in who you can serve.

Shifting your thinking from one-to-one service offerings to one-to-many product and service offerings can quickly take your business to new levels of success. The simple act of creating a marketing funnel can help move this process along by giving you an inexpensive medium for promoting those new programs, products, and services. In some cases, you can see immediate results (like if you send an email promotion and start getting orders right away).

Once you have a solid (and steadily growing!) newsletter community who is already interested in what you have to say, they'll be excited about your new offerings. After all, if you share all of this great free content month after month, they can only imagine what your PAID products will contain!

If you have a thriving community of "fans" of your business, there's really no limit to what you can do, as long as you continue to listen to your community and keep a good handle on what they want and need from you.

Let People "Test" Your Services With Little to No Commitment

When a prospective client first stumbles onto your website, chances are good that he or she WILL NOT hire you on the spot. It would be nice if things worked that way, but they just don't (in most cases).

For the most part, hiring professional help can be pricey and even intimidating for some people, especially if you work virtually and never have the chance to meet your clients face to face. How do they know you are who you say you are and you'll do what you say you'll do (this goes back to the know, like, and trust factor we talked about earlier)? How do they know that you won't just take their money and run?

A great way to prove to prospects just how awesome you are is to let them test out your products and services at little to no charge or obligation. Most often, this is accomplished with the downloading of a free report or the purchase of a low-cost e-book. From there, once the prospect gets a better feel for the quality of your products, he or she will be more likely to take the next step to actually working with you.

Here's an example of a gradual journey people might take to working with you:

- Free report/e-zine/teleseminar
- $27 e-book
- $150 group program
- $500 monthly service program

Here's another bonus to letting prospects "test" you out: your products and group programs will serve to educate prospects to the true value of your services in addition to establishing you as the expert in your niche. When they are ready to move forward with you on a one-on-one basis, here's a likely scenario of what will happen:

- The client seeks you out through phone or email
- The client says he is ready to move forward with your monthly service program
- The client asks how to get started
- The client asks how to pay for the program

Notice that there's no pushing or hard selling of your services; your marketing funnel has authentically attracted the people you're meant to serve and moved them naturally to working with you!

Chapter 2: Find the Right Message

Many small business owners underestimate the importance of taking the time to create an effective website. Oftentimes, they'll spend all their time (or money) on the design of a site and then throw together the content as an afterthought.

BIG MISTAKE!

While design and content should work hand-in-hand, and there are elements of design that can help you increase your results (a subject worthy of its own book), the content of your website is what will ultimately decide your success or failure. This is because if you don't hone in on the right message for your target market, you won't attract their attention, and they'll just click away from your site without taking any action whatsoever. Which leads me to our first action step on the next page.

First and foremost, you need to find out what burning problems your target market most needs help solving. What is keeping them up at night, and how can you make their lives easier/more enjoyable/more successful?

Surveying your target audience

The easiest way to get this information is to survey your potential clients. You have to find out what's bothering them, what they really want to learn and what they are dying to improve in their personal and professional lives. Rather than just guessing, you'll get much better results if you get this info straight from the source. Sounds complicated, but it's actually very simple if you have access to a fair number of members in your target market (and if you don't, you might want to reconsider whether your target market is right for you), either through a newsletter list, an online networking forum, or something similar.

What you'll do is create a survey of five to seven pointed questions that you can use to get insight straight from your potential clients. You can learn what's bothering them, what they're struggling with and how you can help them solve their problems.

For example, if you're a relationship coach who helps single women find their soul mates, you would look for a networking group that is full of single women searching for Mr. Right and invite them to take a short survey (it helps if you're already an active member so that people at that forum know you or at least recognize your name). Be sure to offer them a gift for their time, like a free e-book that might be of interest to them. Another tactic that I've used successfully is to enter all respondents into a contest to win a copywriting service package. The relationship coach in the above example could give an in-depth consultation to one winner, for instance.

For the actual survey set-up, there are a few ways to go about getting it up and running. One option is a free service called www.surveymonkey.com, which I haven't tried myself but have heard is fairly simple to use to create a basic survey that you can post on your website. I would recommend setting up a separate page for the survey, and then you can post a link to that page on the thread you post to your networking forum asking members to take your survey. If you have a newsletter list, most of the autoresponder programs out there, like AWeber and iContact, have a survey option that makes it really easy to create and send surveys without setting up a separate page on your website, and then you can view and/or print out the results at any time. If your autoresponder program doesn't have a survey option, send an email with a link back to the page on your website where the survey is posted.

When you're putting together the questions for your survey, try to include a mix of multiple choice and short-answer questions that don't take too long to answer but will give you a good amount of insight into your target market.

Profitable Newsletters

On the following page, you'll find an example of one of my previous surveys. As you will see, I included a mix of open-ended and multiple-choice questions – and I got some eye-opening responses as a result. Some answers confirmed my beliefs of what my target market was searching for, but others highlighted issues that I hadn't even known were problems for my prospects.

1. Which of the following services would you consider outsourcing (or have you outsourced)? Please check all that apply.

   a. Website copywriting

   b. Article writing

   c. Press release writing

   d. Blog post writing

   e. E-book writing

2. Have you ever worked with a copywriter? Why or why not?

3. Do you have any of the following reservations about working with a copywriter? Please check all that apply.

   a. I can't trust a stranger with my confidential ideas

   b. I can't afford professional copywriting services

   c. I don't know how to find a reputable copywriter

   d. I don't have time to look for a good copywriter

   e. I'd rather just figure out how to write good copy myself

4. What do you struggle with most when it comes to marketing your business?

What questions will you ask?

1. _____

   _____

   _____

2. _____

   _____

   _____

3. _____

   _____

   _____

When you launch your survey, be sure to include a timeframe for receiving answers to avoid procrastination from your prospects. You can send out the survey and tell readers that you'll be announcing a winner (if you're running a contest) in two weeks or that you're only going to give copies of your e-book (or whatever else you're giving away) to the first 50 responders, and, after that, you're shutting the survey down.

Review your survey results

Once you've finished your survey, it's time to review the results. Sit down with a pen/pencil and a piece of paper, and start jotting down responses to your open-ended questions. Try to group them together in like "categories." So, if I had responses that looked like the following:

1. I don't know how to find clients
2. I need more clients
3. I don't have enough clients,

I would group those into one category of "getting clients" and then add three tally marks to show three results in that category. Here's what a completed chart might look like:

Marketing struggles	# of responses
Getting clients	3
Finding time to do it all	10
Becoming known as an expert	5
Finding the right words to appeal to my target market	8

When you finish your survey, you can use the chart below to track and study your own responses.

Struggles	# of responses

Now, circle the most commonly mentioned struggles. Congratulations – you've just honed in on the most common problems that your target market faces; now it's time to turn those struggles into opportunities to highlight your services as the solution to their most pressing problems!

Turning problems into solutions

There's something very fulfilling about being able to solve people's problems, and as a service provider, you have the opportunity to change your clients' lives on a daily basis!

There's really nothing better than using your skills to make an impact on someone else's life. If you can learn how to effectively communicate your message, you will have a greater chance of successfully reaching those you're meant to serve.

To accomplish that goal, just take the problems that you uncovered in the previous pages and write down how your products and services solve those problems. In other words, in this step you're honing in on the benefits of your products and services, and then you will highlight those benefits in all of your marketing materials, your product and service positioning, and even your branding.

If you capture all of the information in one handy chart, your solutions – a.k.a. the major benefits of working with you – should become very clear.

Below, you'll find an example of my solutions chart.

Problem	Product/Service	Solution/Benefit
Getting clients	Customized website copywriting	The right message can help you attract your ideal clients
Becoming known as an expert	Done-for-you email newsletters	Regular, well-written newsletter articles show that you're at the top of your field
No time to do it all	Done-for-you marketing packages	Takes all the time, hassle, and guesswork out of marketing your business

What does yours look like?

Problem	Product/Service	Solution/Benefit

Case study: Why it pays to hone in on the right message

When I first started using email marketing 2 years ago, I didn't have a highly targeted list, so the results of my email marketing were inconsistent. Once I had a highly targeted list, the results happened within a week.

I have used email marketing campaigns to schedule free Niche Attraction Strategy Sessions to help people on my list get clear on their niche. I've had tremendous results with this, resulting in many new coaching clients. I would absolutely recommend that other entrepreneurs not only use email marketing in their business but take the time to get the right message across to their readers.

 Cindy Schulson is a Niche Attraction Expert. She has developed a step-by-step system that helps solo entrepreneurs find and attract their ideal niche so they can market themselves authentically and get faster results. Get a copy of her free report, "Ten Steps to Finding and Attracting Your Ideal Niche" at http://www.attractyourniche.com.

Chapter 3: Create a Solid Foundation for Your Marketing Funnel

Now that you have a good handle on what your marketing message will be, it's time to create the foundation for your marketing funnel – your business website.

If you already have a website, please don't skip over this section; chances are, you can still pick up some pointers to help you get better results.

If you don't yet have a website and have no idea how to get your business online, there's a great report called "Discover the Freedom: 5 Simple Steps to Create & Promote a Wordpress Website" that you can download for free at www.webcentricwebdesign.com. (Full disclosure: this web design website is co-owned by myself and Wordpress web designer Darlene Victoria Gonzalez. But trust me when I say that this report contains everything – and I do mean EVERYTHING – you need to know about taking your business online. Bonus if you're operating on a shoestring budget and want to learn how to get a fully functional website with little to no upfront fees.)

For the purposes of this book, I'm going to assume that you already know how to design your site – or have your site designed for you. We're going to focus instead on the content. There are 5 basic pages that most professional service websites contain. Of course, everyone's website needs are different, so you may have more or less pages (at the time of this writing, my website – including the "behind-the-scenes" pages that most people don't see – has 60 pages – yes, **60!**), and you may choose to name your pages differently than what is suggested here. Go for it! My goal is only to give you a frame of reference to get your creativity flowing.

Read on for the 5 basic pages your website will likely consist of:

Home page

This one probably won't change. It's an old standby for pretty much any website, and it's needed to share a basic overview of your business, who you serve, and how you can help them. The home page is, arguably, the *most important page* of your website because it is where most visitors will "land" on your site. When they type in your website URL (for example, www.abc-company.com), they'll see your home page. For that fact alone, it will likely get the most traffic and, therefore, the most visibility of all your pages. When you're creating the content for your website, the home page is where you should spend 90% of your time (no exaggeration!).

Here's a sample format that you can follow when putting your home page copy together:

Attention-grabbing headline

Introduction paragraph

Statement of benefits – often in the form of a bulleted list such as this one:

- Get clients
- Establish expertise
- Save time

Statement of features/services – in another bulleted list:

- Website copywriting
- Done-for-you newsletters
- Done-for-you marketing package

Call-to-action – such as, call me at 555-1234 for a free consultation

---

About page

As the title suggests, on this page you'll share more information about your company. As a solo entrepreneur, this page will mostly be about you, but it's a good idea to keep it somewhat professional. That's not to say you can't throw in a paragraph about personal interests and/or aspects of your personal life that led you to pursuing your passions – especially if that information could help form a connection with your target market. For example, if you're targeting work-at-home moms and you left your corporate job to start a home-based business when your child was born, that information could increase the likeability factor with your target market – so feel free to shout it from the rooftops!

One idea for an impressive, informative About page is to write in an interview-style Q&A format.

Here are some questions you might consider including:

1) How did you become a (insert title here, i.e. Client Attracting Web Copy Specialist, in my case)?
2) How will we work together?
3) What is the time investment involved with your services/programs?
4) Do you accept credit cards?
5) Can I contact you if I want to learn more?

This is just a sampling of potential questions; to pick up a few more (and get examples of answers), check out my About page at http://writeassociate.com/about-us/.

Who I Work With page

The Who I Work With page can be used to pre-qualify your ideal clients, saving you the time of trying to retain prospects that aren't a good fit for your business. When you include this page on your website, you will attract the people you're meant to serve while at the same time disqualifying less-than-ideal clients. I know, the thought of purposely turning potential clients away may be a bit scary, but trust me – it's best for you *and* your non-ideal clients. You can move on to working with the people who are going to get the most benefit and value from your products and services, which serves two purposes: 1) you will gain lifelong customers, 2) they will be so thrilled that they'll spread the word to their friends and colleagues – who are also most likely your ideal clients (since birds of a feather do tend to flock together). The potential clients that you disqualify can then move on to find solutions that will work better for them and that they will get more satisfaction from. Everybody wins!

Here's an example of a format you can follow:

Introductory paragraph

List of identifying characteristics

Launch into a series of benefits statements

Let the client "see" the better life that is waiting for them

Disqualify/describe people who need not apply

Call-to-action

To see this in action, check out
http://writeassociate.com/who-we-help/.

Services/How I Help page

The How I Help page (could also be called Services) should offer a detailed description of your service programs, along with the results clients can expect through working with you.

If you have different service packages, you can either list them here, or you can use the How I Help page to go into detail on the benefits of your services, and discuss the service packages themselves in detail on a separate page.

This is how my website is currently structured (yes, I say "currently" because my website is constantly evolving and changing as I try new things).

Currently, my How I Help page says the following:

We can help you get more money, more free time, more fulfillment and more FUN from your service business

On to the good stuff...what you can expect to get by working with us.

Exciting benefits of working with us

If you found yourself nodding your head in agreement to

the statements on our Who We Help page, you're a great candidate for our programs! After working with us, you will have a strong web presence that will result in:

- More clients (translation: **more money**)
- Less effort (translation: **more free time**)
- Regular, consistent results from your marketing
- **More fun & greater fulfillment** from your business

Cool features of our programs

By finishing our website creation & promotion programs, you'll walk away with:

- A better understanding of your ideal client & how to reach them effectively
- A website that draws potential clients in and causes them to take specific action (like signing up for your e-newsletter or contacting you for more info)
- A great-looking website design that you'll be excited to show off!
- A step by step, easy to maintain plan that puts your marketing on auto-pilot
- Increased credibility with your target market
- A solid follow-up program to help you stay in touch with people who are interested in working with you
- A special offer that captures attention and helps you grow your newsletter list
- And so much more

Our philosophy on business websites & internet marketing

Here at The Write Associate, we believe that a great business website should be the hub of a self-employed service provider's online presence. After all, you can pump out articles for article marketing, create podcasts, publish videos, (all of which are solid internet marketing methods, by the way) etc. until you're blue in the face, but if you're driving traffic to a website that doesn't convince potential clients to take action, you're just wasting a lot of time and effort.

We believe that the components of a client-attracting web presence for service providers include (in order of importance):

1) A solid understanding of your ideal clients, what they need and how you specifically can help them solve their problems
2) A client-attracting website that causes visitors to take action
3) An easy-to-follow, results-oriented marketing plan that helps you bring clients in almost automatically month after month

Our step-by-step programs will give you all of the above, and then some!

Our satisfaction guarantee

We don't rest until our clients are thrilled with our work. Whether it takes one revision or twenty, rest assured that you'll love the finished product!

What makes us stand out from other copywriting companies?

So, the question of the day is: "Why should I hire you over the gazillion other copywriting & internet marketing companies out there?" We're so glad you asked!

• Because we primarily work with self-employed service

professionals, we know what works and what doesn't work when it comes to website design and internet marketing.

• Our team contains a group of savvy website designers and experienced marketing consultants that work together to make sure your website gets the best possible results.

• We've pooled our combined knowledge and resources to help you get more bang for your buck.

Our sole focus is making sure you succeed

Whether you're just getting your business started or have been around the block a few times, we are 100% dedicated to helping you create a client-attracting web presence that will launch your business forward and help you get results as quickly as possible.

Next, please **check out samples of our work and find out what clients are saying about our services**.

And then my Services page goes into more detail about my different programs, what they involve, and what clients can expect when working with me.

However, as I mentioned earlier, you can also choose to have one Services page that touches on the benefits of your programs and then goes into detail about each service program, all on one page. How you choose to structure your site is entirely up to you, so feel free to choose the style that works best for you.

Contact page

The Contact page is the simplest of your web pages because all it contains is your basic contact information, a contact form (if you should choose to go that route), and perhaps an introductory paragraph. You don't have to get all fancy or detailed here; you can simply start your Contact page with something like:

"Thanks for your interest in (your business name)! I'm looking forward to connecting with you. Please use one of the methods below to contact me, and I'll get back to you as soon as possible."

What will your Contact page say?

_____

_____

_____

_____

It's best to include as many ways to contact you as possible. If you work from your home office, you may not want to include your physical address (although a P.O. Box is fine), and you can also throw a few spaces into your email address to discourage spammers.

Example: Instead of info@writeassociate.com, type out info @ writeassociate.com.

Whether or not you include your phone number is up to you; I don't typically take calls when they come in, preferring to return voicemails all at one time, but I do provide my office phone number on my website in case someone wants to reach me that way.

I also include my Twitter, Facebook, and Skype information so people can follow/contact me that way if they'd like. The bottom line is that you want to give people options to contact you within their own comfort zones – some people prefer email, others prefer phone calls, so you just want to make sure that you're as accessible as possible to potential clients.

Chapter 4: Craft an Outstanding Giveaway Offer

Back when email newsletters first came about, you might have gotten away with just announcing your newsletter and inviting people to join – and the sheer novelty of receiving information on certain topics directly in one's email inbox was enough to get people to sign up.

Nowadays, however, people have thousands, if not millions, of choices when it comes to email newsletters on topics ranging from parenting to home improvement to small business marketing, so you have to work harder to entice new subscribers.

The best way to do this is to create a free giveaway that people can instantly download – in exchange for their name and email address, of course.

But it can't be just any old giveaway – it has to be irresistible to your target market.

For example, if you're a business coach, you could put together a free report called, "5 Ways to Double Your Profits This Year."

An internet marketing virtual assistant could create a video walking people through the process of setting up or customizing a Twitter profile.

My friend and colleague Darlene Victoria Gonzalez, who specializes in increasingly-popular multi-media services like podcast and video production, gives away a free audio download called "The R.A.P. Report – 3 Tips to Help Improve Your Speaking for Audio and Video Productions." (Visit http://yourtrueharmony.com/ if you'd like to check it out.)

Choosing the right format

So, as you can see, if you hate to write, there's good news: Your free giveaway does NOT have to be a written report.

It also doesn't have to be long and complicated. Here are some ideas of a free giveaway you could put together:

- A 5-page written report containing top 10 tips
- A 15-minute audio report that teaches people how to do one specific thing

- A 15-minute video that shows people how to accomplish a certain task
- A 5-day e-course that teaches people the fundamentals of your subject matter

What will you put together?

_____

_____

Now that you have an idea of the format you'll use, take a moment to brainstorm topics for your free giveaway. If you're not sure what people want to learn about, don't guess – ask them! You could visit networking forums that your target market frequents and find out the questions that people are asking over and over again, or post a new thread straight out asking people what they want to learn about. Another option is to think back on the last few prospects who contacted you and jot down the questions that they asked you about your products and services. If you can identify a need and then find a way to fill it, you'll be well on your way to building a thriving community of hot prospects – a.k.a. a solid newsletter list.

Brainstorming free giveaway topics

On the following page, you'll find a brainstorming map that will help you choose potential topics. You'll start with a broad idea – such as Getting Clients – and just start jotting down any other thoughts that spring to mind. Don't censor yourself; even if it doesn't seem relevant, you might be able to use that idea at some point down the road. The point is to get as many thoughts down onto paper as possible; you can sift through them later to pick out the "winners."

Please take a minute now to take a look at my brainstorming map example below, and then you'll have space for your own brainstorming map.

Brainstorming map

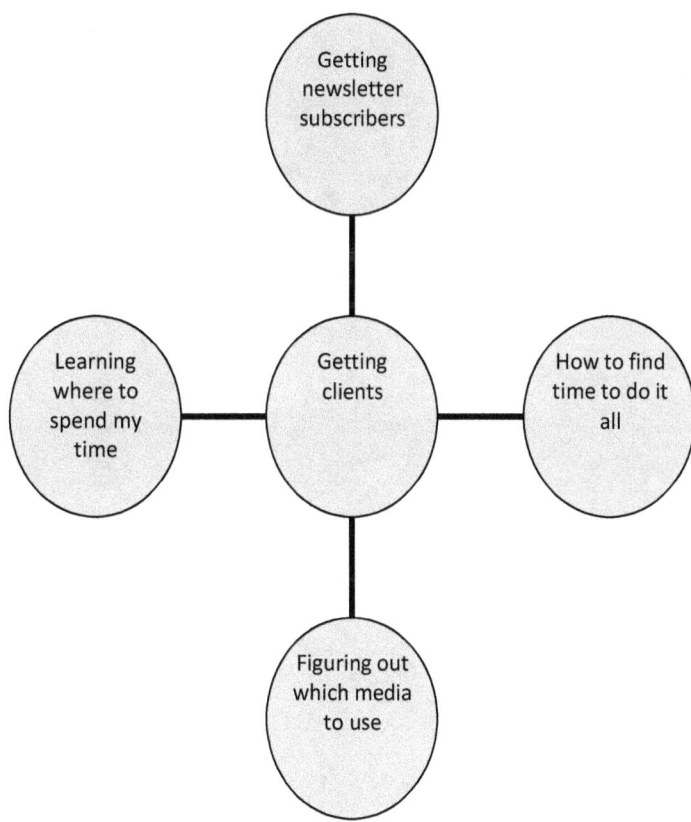

Notice that "Getting clients" is the main, or focal, point, and everything else springs from there. People that I surveyed wanted to get more clients, but they didn't know where to start or how to spend their marketing time for optimal results. Based on this, I outlined a series of products, the first of which you're holding in your hand right now.

This simple brainstorming exercise brought to mind a few other products that I plan to create as well, so it served several purposes.

Use the blank brainstorming map below to jot down some of your own potential free giveaway topics.

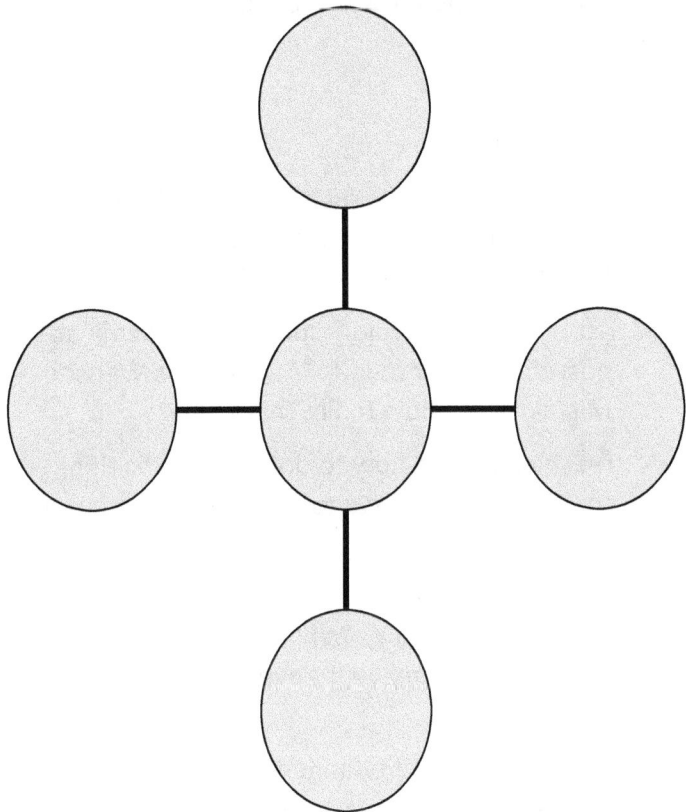

Determine your angle

Once you have your main topic, you'll need to hone in on how you're going to approach it, or what angle you're going to take. Every subject can be approached from a variety of angles, so you could actually take the same main topic and spin it into several free giveaways – or even use them in your other marketing efforts by turning the unused angles into articles, videos, podcasts, teleseminars, etc. The possibilities are quite literally endless, once you open the floodgates and let the ideas come crashing in!

Common angles to take are:

- Top 10 tips sheets – such as one of my former free reports, "Top 10 Tips for Writing Web Copy that Will Explode Your Sales!"

- List of things to avoid – such as a teleseminar I co-hosted last year called, "7 Disastrous Website Mistakes and How to Fix Them"

- Teaching people how to do one specific thing – for example, "3 Ways to Get More Newsletter Subscribers"

- Educating readers on the benefits of a particular topic – for instance, "Why you should see an optometrist every year - even if your eyesight is perfect!"

- Warn people about dangers they may not be aware of – such as, "5 Long-Term Health Effects of Living in a Moldy Home"

Put together an outstanding title

Last but certainly not least, you'll want to spend a good chunk of time putting together the title for your free giveaway. It needs to capture attention while also communicating the who, what, and why of your giveaway.

By that, I mean:

Who – who is your giveaway for?

What – what is your giveaway about?

Why – why should readers take the time to download and read/listen to/watch your giveaway?

Here are some potential titles that you might be able to use for your free giveaway (depending on the topic, of course!):

- "5 Steps to Doubling Your Company's Bottom Line This Year"
- "The Entrepreneur's Step-by-Step Guide to Twitter Profiles that Sell Your Services"
- "How to Train Your Dog in 30 Days or Less"
- "The Work-at-Home Mom's Guide to Increased Productivity"

Often, the why is implied – doubling your company's bottom line will lead to more money for the owner, as will Twitter profiles that sell your services. Most every dog owner wants to know how to quickly train their dog to be more obedient, and work-at-home moms often struggle with juggling their many responsibilities.

There are several proven formulas for creating winning titles. Following are just a few of them, any one of which can be used to create a compelling title:

1. Lead with the word "Introducing," which is always an attention-grabber. Example: "Introducing a Brand-New Way to Grow Your Newsletter List!"

2. Write as if you're announcing exciting news, such as "Announcing a Better Method to Find the Love of Your Life!"

3. Get personal with a compelling story, like "How I Grew My Profits by 200% in Just 6 Months."

4. Begin with "How to," an ever-popular phrase in advertising headlines. Example: "How to Lose 10 Pounds of Water Weight in 10 Days."

You don't have to get overly witty with your title – sometimes the plain and simple facts are actually better, but you do need to be convincing enough to attract interest from potential subscribers, so take the time to put some thought into your title. Once you have a few good ideas, run them by friends and colleagues to get their thoughts. If you can, get feedback from members of your target market to find out if they would be interested in a giveaway of this nature. Would it grab their interest enough to subscribe to your newsletter?

With that being said, don't stress too much...if your giveaway flops, you can always experiment with other titles to find one that will bring in new subscribers. This isn't a one-shot deal, and you can always make changes if you're not happy with the results.

Take a moment now to brainstorm several potential titles for your free giveaway, and record them here:

1. _____

_____

2. _____

_____

3. _____

_____

4. _____

_____

5. _____

_____

After you run your top title picks past your friends and colleagues, write the winner here:

_____

_____

Chapter 5: Create Your Free Giveaway "System"

When you have a free giveaway, there are a few steps people should go through:

1. They will visit your free giveaway opt-in page.
2. After subscribing, they should be automatically sent to either a thank you page or an upsell page.

Let's talk about those in more detail now.

The free giveaway opt-in page

You may have noticed that the people who enjoy massive mailing lists almost always have at least one page (and sometimes entire websites!) devoted to their free giveaway and/or e-newsletter. With the amount of information overload and time starvation out there, people are getting more and more particular about who they let into their inbox and what they spend time reading, so you have to convince them to sign up for something, even when it's 100% free information.

Preferably, your opt-in page will be a landing page completely separate from your website, as in the screenshot below:

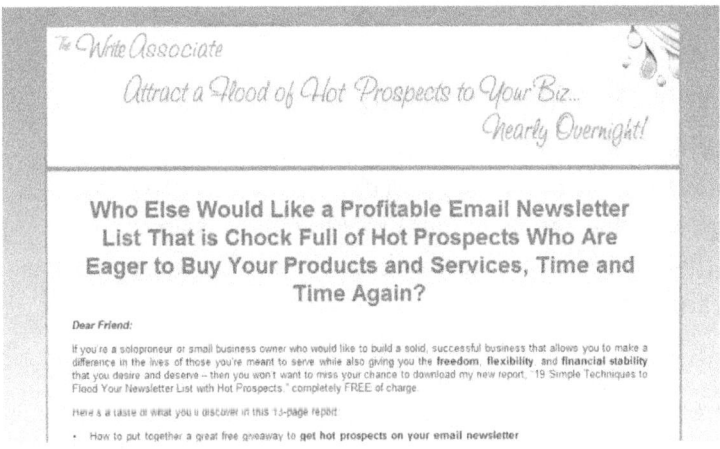

This opt-in page requires the creation of a landing page that matches the branding you have on your website, so if you don't have the resources to hire a landing page designer (like the fantastic team we have over at Webcentric Web Design), you can just add a page to your website, which might then look like something the image on the following page.

Writing the opt-in page copy

What's really more important is the content that you have on this opt-in page. While I don't have the space to go into the details of what makes a great sales page (that's a topic for another book!), here's a template you can follow:

Headline: Here is where you reach out to your target audience and grab their attention with a strong hook. Tell the audience exactly what you have for them, and why they should keep reading. Refer to the title tips in Chapter 4 – those will also work for headlines. Example:

Small Business Owners: Would You Like To Discover How To Get More Clients Through Your Website?

Greeting: If you're speaking to a specific group, use an identifying characteristic, like "Dear Business Coach." Otherwise, use "Dear Friend."

Opening paragraph: Tell readers who you are and why you're writing to them. Basically, give them the nutshell version of your message. Here's an example from my opt-in page:

If you're a solo entrepreneur or small business owner who would like to build a solid, successful business that allows you to make a difference in the lives of those you're meant to serve while also giving you the freedom, flexibility, and financial stability that you desire and deserve – then you won't want to miss your chance to download my new report, "19 Simple Techniques to Flood Your Newsletter List with Hot Prospects," completely FREE of charge.

Body: Now you'll get into the meat of your content, where you'll give all the juicy details that will entice readers to grab your free giveaway and get on your newsletter list. You can start by saying something like, "Here's what you'll discover in this 15-page report:" (changing the page count to match your report, of course), followed by a bulleted list of 3 or 4 teaser statements, which will give readers just a taste of what they will learn in your free giveaway.

Here's an example of my bulleted list:

- How to put together a great free giveaway to get people on your email newsletter list (along with a juicy tip that will be music to the ears of all you non-writers out there!)

- One thing you *must* do first if you want to attract scores of hot prospects to your email newsletter list
- When to follow-up with new subscribers and how to urge them to take a specific action – such as buying your paid products or services – without feeling pushy or "sales-y"
- Hot tips to begin building your email newsletter list (all for FREE or very low-cost)

Call-to-action: At this point, you'll invite readers to take a specific action; in this case, that action will be entering their name and email address in the sign-up form in exchange for immediate access to the free giveaway. Tell readers exactly what you want them to do - even if it seems obvious to you. If there's any doubt in their minds, they'll be more likely to click away than to contact you for help – and you've just lost a prospective client.

Add a P.S. at the end of the page: For reasons still unknown, the P.S. at the end of a letter or web page often gets more readership than the body of the page itself. Use this prime space to state your case again, briefly. If you have any glowing testimonials from people who've received your giveaway (hint: you may have to actively seek these out, by asking people you know to review your giveaway and give their feedback), throw one in here – third party endorsements go a LONG way toward convincing people to request whatever you're offering.

Thank you/upsell pages

Once new subscribers have requested your free giveaway, they should be taken to either a thank you page or an upsell page.

The thank you page

A thank you page is exactly as it sounds: a page thanking new subscribers for requesting your free giveaway. It can also do several other things:

1. Give the subscriber specific instructions, such as checking their email for the download link
2. Tell new subscribers what to expect, such as a confirmation email where they'll need to click a link to confirm their subscription before they will get their free giveaway
3. Invite subscribers to tell their friends about your giveaway

On the following page, you'll find an example of my current thank you page.

> **Thanks for requesting your free copy of my new report, which will reveal 19 simple techniques to flood your newsletter list with hot prospects!**
>
> A confirmation email has been sent to your email address. Please click the link to confirm your request and you'll immediately receive the link to your free report. Don't forget to click the link or we won't be able to send your free report. Also, to make sure that you get your report and future offers, please be sure to whitelist our emails.
>
> **Click here to Tweet about this free report!**
>
> If you have any questions or concerns, please contact me.

Notice the part where I invite new subscribers to tweet about the report? This link is especially helpful because a) it gives people useful Twitter content (something many of us struggle to find on a regular basis!) to share with their followers and b) it gives you exposure to more potential subscribers. That's definitely my definition of a win-win situation!

Creating the thank you page

If you are using a Wordpress website or otherwise have the ability to insert HTML code into your website, here's the code you will insert onto your thank you page:

```
<a title="Click to share this post on Twitter"
href="http://twitter.com/home?status=Just got my free
report from @writeassociate re: building a profitable
newsletter list. Grab ur copy here:
http://ow.ly/ul1o"><strong>Click here to Tweet about
this free report!</strong></a>
```

The yellow (light-colored) highlighted portion will be replaced by your particular message – just be sure that it stays within Twitter's 140 character limit (I usually copy and paste it into a Twitter message field to make sure), and don't forget to include a link to your free giveaway's opt-in page (you can use a free service like www.tinyurl.com or www.bit.ly to shorten your URL so it doesn't take up as many characters – that's why my URL reads as http://ow.ly/ul1o instead of my much longer, regular URL).

The pink (dark-colored) highlighted portion above is what readers will see on the page – feel free to use it as is or tweak it to fit your needs.

Finally, I wrapped up my thank you page with an invitation to contact me, including a link to my contact page, if subscribers had any questions or concerns.

And that about wraps up the thank you page. It's very simple to put up (you'll find even more details on the "technical aspect" of linking your thank you page to the subscription process in Chapter 6) but can leave subscribers with a comfortable experience – rather than just leaving them wondering what on earth they should expect next. Bonus: if you invite them to spread the word, you could get even more new subscribers out of the deal!

The upsell page

Instead of sending new subscribers to a thank you page, you could opt to send them to an upsell page, which would promote a particular product or service, often one that is related to the free giveaway but that requires an investment (of either time or money) from them.

For instance, let's say that you're a marketing coach who specializes in helping brick-and-mortar small business owners build a strong online presence. What you can do is put together a 10-page report giving an overview of the five critical steps needed to take a business online. Your upsell page could promote any of the following paid products:

- A 50-page e-book that dives deeper into the above-mentioned steps
- A pre-recorded teleseminar – co-hosted by yourself and a web design or copywriting expert – about building an effective website, sold with the recording and written transcript

- A group training program or home study course that covers the topic with more detail and step-by-step assistance

Conversely, you could also offer something else for free – specifically, a free consultation with you to talk about their struggles and see whether you're the solution to their most pressing problems. In my experience, I've seen two popular ways to approach the free consultation:

1. A getting-to-know-each-other type of call, where you don't necessarily answer specific questions related to your area of expertise but rather determine whether your products and services are a good fit for the potential client.

2. A free services session, where you actually perform a certain amount of services – such as a free coaching session or a free hour of Virtual Assistant services – that is designed to give potential clients a taste of your services and leave them eager for more.

I've used both of these in my business and would like to issue a word of caution: if you try tactic #2 and haven't either pre-qualified your prospects or honed up on your selling skills to close people after the "trial" period, you might find yourself giving a lot of your time to tire-kickers - those people who are always just looking for a freebie - and gaining very few paying clients.

With that being said, feel free to try both options in your business as well to see which, if either, will work best for you.

Putting together the upsell page

The upsell page is similar in format to the opt-in page, with just a few minor – but important! – differences. I won't repeat the instructions for the copywriting sections, since those were already covered in the previous section on opt-in pages, so please refer to those for further instructions. Otherwise, here's the format you can follow:

Headline

Greeting

Opening paragraph

Body

Offer: Here's where your upsell page starts to get different from an opt-in page for a free giveaway. On an upsell page for a paid product, you will need to state your price – *after* you've loaded the reader up with reasons to buy your product, that is. If you'd like, you can offer a discount for subscribers – and this is where you would present your special discount.

Call-to-action: After you've stated your offer, take a sentence or two to reinforce the major benefits of your product. Then give the reader a reason to buy now – such as limited space in your program or a specific deadline to the discount (for example: two weeks from the date of their download). And then – this is the most important part – ASK the reader to make the purchase! So simple, yet so many people skip this all-important step and lose out on many purchases because of

---

it. This request can be as simple as saying, "Click the Buy Now button below to place your order now!"

Add a guarantee: A guarantee is nearly essential for online sales; because people can't actually hold the product in their hands, there's a greater perceived risk that you – some unknown, faceless company – will take their money and run with it. They might also think that maybe you'll give them the product, but it will be worthless junk, and they will have wasted their money. So, here's a million-dollar secret for you: Include a generous guarantee, and you'll find yourself making more sales. Possibly a LOT more sales, just for taking some of the risk off the potential buyer's hands so they can feel better about making a purchase from you.

Don't forget the P.S.

There you have it: a simple format for an upsell page for your paid products and services.

If you put this free giveaway system in place, you will increase your chances of converting subscribers from passive receivers (of your free giveaway) to paying customers of your products and services.

Remember: If they requested your free giveaway, they're already interested in what you have to say; catch them while the desire for more on your topic of expertise is still hot, and you'll skyrocket your success rate.

Chapter 6: The Follow-Up System

Now that you have a strong foundation for creating your marketing funnel, it's time to actually set up your follow-up system.

One thing you should NOT do is try to handle it all yourself. By that, I mean using your own email account to actually send the emails, hand-delivering your free giveaway to each new subscriber, etc. Fortunately, there are several amazing programs out there that you can use to handle the entire process for you automatically, which means that once you finish the initial groundwork, your work will be done. You can just sit back and watch the new subscribers come pouring in!

The technical aspect behind your follow-up system capturing does require the purchase of an autoresponder program, which is basically a monthly service that allows you to put sign-up forms on your website and then, once a client enters their name and email address, the autoresponder automatically sends the recipient an email that you customized in advance. So, when new subscribers sign up for your free giveaway/newsletter, they will automatically get a pre-written email that welcomes them to your newsletter community and provides instructions for downloading their free gift. We'll talk more about setting up the welcome email in Step 5 on the following pages.

Checking out the options

There are several popular autoresponder options out there, including Aweber, iContact, and MadMimi.

While Aweber is perhaps the most popular option (right now, at least), they're also the priciest. As of the time of this writing, pricing was as follows:

- Aweber - $19/month for a basic plan of 0-500 subscribers, then $29/month for 501-2,500 subscribers

- iContact - $9.95/month for 0-250 subscribers, then $14/month for 251-500 subscribers

- MadMimi - $5/month for 0-100 subscribers (the basic plan is actually free, but you have to pay $5 for the autoresponder option), then $13 for up to 500 subscribers

I personally have used all three services and have noticed little difference among them. I tend to prefer iContact, but that's because I've used it the most. To be fair,

Aweber does have some cool extra features, such as pop-up web forms that invite people to request your free giveaway, that I haven't noticed on the other programs. I suppose the best route would be to take a closer look at each of your options and what you get for your money before making your final decision.

Keep in mind, when looking at pricing, that if autoresponders are used correctly, they can more than make up for their own cost. In the next chapter, we'll talk about using your autoresponder program to send bulk emails to your newsletter list on a regular basis.

For now, just know that you can use any of these programs to capture contact information and distribute your free giveaway and future promotions to subscribers.

Setting up your autoresponder

Although each autoresponder is different in terms of the set-up process, there are some basic fundamentals that we can cover here, so let's begin walking through the steps of setting up your autoresponder, shall we?

Step 1: Create an account

Depending on the autoresponder you choose, there will be different verbiage for you to create your account. For example, on MadMimi you'll click the tab that says, "Sign up." Aweber has an option called "Order," and currently with iContact, you can sign up for a free trial directly on their home page.

From there, follow the instructions to create an account.

Step 2: Set up your sign-up form

This step will also vary depending on the autoresponder service you choose. In iContact, for instance, you'll look under the My Contacts tab for the Sign-up Forms option, and then scroll down to the button that says "Create a New Sign-up Form." On the other hand, the sign-up forms in MadMimi are actually called web forms, so you'll look for something like that.

Enter your first name and primary email address below to instantly discover how to flood your service business with hot prospects!

Click here to learn more.

- First Name

- Email

- = Required Field

Submit

PS: You will also receive a free subscription to our bi-weekly e-zine, Copywriting to Get Clients (a $97 value). We will never rent, sell, or share your information with anyone else, period!

In each of the autoresponder programs that I've worked with, creating a sign-up form is very simple – with no technical knowledge required. Don't worry about not knowing HTML code – you won't need it! Just follow the instructions your chosen autoresponder gave you to create your sign-up form, which might look something like the image above when all is said and done.

Keep in mind, though, that your sign-up form will likely be different based on your free giveaway, whether you include a photo of your free giveaway like I did, and the forms provided by your autoresponder program.

The most important things to have here are: a compelling statement about your free giveaway, the fields to collect their first name and email address, and a privacy notice (mine is at the bottom, under the Submit button) promising not to rent, sell, or share their contact information with anyone else.

Step 3: Link to your upsell page

Your autoresponder program should have the availability to send subscribers to a new page once they've signed up. In iContact, this is called the Success URL. Here's where you'll enter the URL address of your thank you/upsell page (such as http://www.writeassociate.com/thank-you-free-report-request, which is my current Success URL). This might also be called the subscription confirmation page.

Step 4: Upload your free report to your website

You may need to contact your website host for assistance with this part, but if you use a host that offers the user-friendly cPanel, you'll just go into your File Manager, create a new folder called Downloads, double-click the Downloads folder, and then walk through the steps of uploading your free giveaway (start by clicking the Upload icon and then follow the instructions given).

When your file is uploaded, you should then be able to direct readers to:

YourWebsiteAddress.com/Downloads/YourFileName

So if your website URL is BecomeACoach.com, and your free giveaway was saved as "5_Ways_To_Coach_Others_To_Success.pdf" then your URL would be: BecomeACoach.com/Downloads/5_Ways_To_Coach_Others_To_Success.pdf.

Just remember that this link IS case-sensitive, so if you saved the file as "5_ways_to_coach_others_to_success.pdf," that's how it will appear in your URL.

Step 5: Customize your welcome message

Your welcome message will be sent out to new subscribers as soon as they confirm their subscription.

On the following page, you'll find an example of my current welcome email that you can use for inspiration when creating your own welcome email.

Subject: Psst - here's that report you've been waiting for!

Thanks for requesting your free copy of my special report, "19 Simple Techniques to Build a Thriving Email List of Hot Prospects!"

Please click here to download your copy.

If you just can't figure out how to attract more clients, rest assured: help is available!

I've put together a unique 6-step program (trust me, you haven't seen anything like this before!) for attracting a flood of hot prospects to your service business and building a profitable website. You can learn more about it during my FREE upcoming teleseminar, which takes place on Tuesday, April 6th. If you're looking to build your own thriving community of hot prospects, you won't want to miss this call!

Click here to register now!

To your success,

Tammi Metzler
www.ClientAttractingWebCopy.com

As you can see, this email serves several purposes:

1. Offers a sincere thank you and a warm welcome to your newsletter community

2. Provides the download link for the free giveaway you promised them

3. Introduces them to an opportunity to try more of your products and services – in the case above, I'm inviting readers to join my free teleseminar, but you can also promote paid products and services that are related to the free giveaway

Feel free to tweak my welcome message to suit your purposes.

To actually get to this part, here's what you will need to do. If you're using iContact, click the Create tab, and then click Create an Autoresponder. Fill out the appropriate info on the first page, and then click Save & Add Message.

From here, simply type your Subject line in the Email Subject field and then either type or copy & paste your email text into the box marked "Create your HTML Email." (Don't let the HTML part fool you – it's super-easy to use. Trust me, I had no HTML knowledge when I first started, and it's still very limited today – but I can still somehow manage to find my way around these forms!)

When you've created your HTML email, scroll down and click the Copy Text button. This step just basically copies your email into the plain-text option for people who can't view HTML emails.

After you have finished this set-up, I would recommend sending a test email to yourself and checking your email to make sure it looks okay before clicking save.

When you're satisfied with the way it looks, save your changes. Be sure to enable your autorespoder, if need be. In iContact, you would do that by clicking the Send tab, then Enable my Autoresponders. Your eligible autoresponders will be listed here, and off to the far right will be two blue arrows. Click those to enable your autoresponders, and you should be good to go!

Chapter 7: Follow Up Consistently

Once you start collecting contact information, what you do with it will make or break your marketing efforts. Those who request your free giveaway have already positioned themselves as people who are interested in what you have to say, which makes them prime candidates for your products and services.

If you don't follow up consistently, however, from within a few days/weeks of their initial sign-up, you run the risk of having subscribers forgetting who you are (and that you provided all of that wonderful information in your free giveaway) and writing you off as a spammer, unsubscribing from your email list and potentially even sending a complaint about your "spamming" actions (yes, this can and does happen!).

On the other hand, if you nurture your newsletter community with consistent, content-rich emails, they will come to see you as the professional resource – and answer to their most pressing problems – that you are.

Not only will you be building the know, like, and trust factor with your current subscribers - who will then be more likely to purchase your products and services - but if you make a strong impression, your subscribers will spread the word about you to their friends and colleagues. Those people will begin subscribing to your newsletter, and before you know it, you'll have a thriving newsletter community full of hot prospects who will be eager to buy your valuable products and services.

Why? Because the people on your mailing list are already interested in what you have to say, and since you're providing all of the high-quality free content, your paid products and services must be 10 times better (and they should be, or word will quickly spread about that as well!). They wanted the information you provided in your free giveaway, and they are hungry for any more information that you can provide on your area of expertise.

Which means that if you can send them tidbits of useful information at least once a month in the form of an e-newsletter (email newsletter), a.k.a. an e-zine (email magazine), your mailing list will also be receptive to promotions of your products, teleseminars, service packages, etc. If you have something that will help them grow their business, lose weight, or whatever you specialize in, you can use your e-newsletter to keep them interested, remind them that you're available, and help them trust that you are just the professional to help them solve their problems!

Choose a publishing schedule

So, how often should you publish your e-newsletter? You'll want to publish *at least* once a month; any less, and you run the risk mentioned earlier of people forgetting who you are and instantly unsubscribing (or worse, proclaiming you a spammer). It's hardly worth the effort of publishing a quality e-newsletter if half your list is going to unsubscribe after each issue.

I've found that the ideal publishing schedule is twice per month – it's enough to keep your name in front of potential prospects without driving them bonkers…or leading to burnout on your end.

If you can't quite commit to two issues per month, however, start with one and once that is going well for you, bump up to two issues.

The key is to choose a regular publishing schedule that your e-newsletter community can count on. So, for example, say that you're going to start off by publishing once a month – pick a day each month that you plan to publish, such as the third Thursday of each month, and **stick to it**!

Publishing regularly does two main things:

1. As previously mentioned, keeps your name in front of potential clients, and

2. Shows that you are dependable and trustworthy (remember the know, like, and trust factor?)

What will your schedule be?

_____

Decide when to send your e-newsletter

There's a lot of speculation out there about which day you should publish your e-newsletter. There's really not much concrete evidence out there, and the stats tend to change month to month, so the bottom line is that you should either do your own testing to see which publishing date your readership responds to, or choose a day that fits best into your schedule and run with it.

I should mention, though, that the time of day you send your e-newsletter will also have an impact on how many people open and read your e-newsletter.

One popular school of thought (again, there's not much research to support or disprove this) is that early morning isn't good for e-newsletters because people are overloaded with emails and will be more likely to delete – or at the very least skip over – those emails that aren't seen as important.

In a blog post published by Aweber, the newsletter publishing company we talked about earlier in this book, they found that the period of 2-3 p.m. EST actually claimed the largest open rates (or amount of people who are opening your e-newsletters). The theory is that during the mid-afternoon period, you're more likely to catch people who are ready for a break – and some leisurely reading – and also that they'll be less frantic with other activities. However, this line of thinking mostly applies to businesspeople; if you target stay-at-home moms, for instance, you might find them to be more receptive to your emails at a completely different time of day.

To test this out for yourself, try sending your e-newsletter out at different times of the day and track your open rates - you can find that information from your e-newsletter publishing company, or you can figure it out for yourself by dividing the number of emails opened by the number of emails sent (so if you have 150 subscribers, you sent 150 emails, and if 25 of them opened your e-newsletter, you would divide 25 by 150 to get 16% - your open rate for that particular e-newsletter issue).

Evaluate your open rates

Typical open rates can range depending on your industry, but according to a report from Aweber, the average open rate for a recent month was 13.6%. If you can average between 20-30%, you're in good shape.

If you can get your open rate above 30%, consider yourself an email marketing rock star!

Use the basic editorial calendar below to track your e-newsletter publishing schedule. You can either circle the day(s) each month you plan to publish or jot down a note in the space below each number. For example, on mine I would circle the 2nd and 4th Tuesday, which is when I publish my e-newsletter. (Hint: I often use the blank space to note my idea for that issue's topic, so you can try that as well if you'd like.) When will you publish your e-newsletter?

Sun.	Mon.	Tues.	Wed.	Thurs.	Fri.	Sat.
1	2	3	4	5	6	7
8	9	10	11	12	13	14
15	16	17	18	19	20	21
22	23	24	25	26	27	28
29	30					

Chapter 8: Don't Reinvent the Wheel

Your weekly/monthly publishing job will be 10 times easier if you create templates that you can plug new content into for each issue. Not only will this save you massive amounts of time, but it will also help with the overwhelm factor – since you're not starting from scratch with each issue, your job won't seem quite so staggering.

You can either have a text e-newsletter or HTML e-newsletter.

Here's an example of a text e-newsletter:

```
Copywriting to Get Clients
Tammi Metzler, Publisher
mailto:tammim@writeassociate.com

<><><><><><><><><><><><><><><><><><><><><>

1) A note from Tammi

-----------------------------------------------------------
```

Hi [fname],

I hope you had an enjoyable and relaxing holiday season! Mine was filled with family, festivities, and some light work, mostly planning for the year to come. I was also looking back at some of the surveys I ran this past year to see if there are any common marketing struggles that I haven't yet touched on, and one thing that was mentioned over and over again was finding the time to get around to all-important marketing tasks.

You were asking me how on earth you were supposed to find time to write when your schedule is already packed. Trust me, I know the feeling...there was quite a while when I struggled to get any marketing done; it was always getting pushed to the side. Seemed like everything else in my life took priority: client work, administrative tasks, strategic planning.

And then the day came that my client projects started coming to an end and suddenly, I found myself scrambling to find clients, *fast*! That's when I learned that if I wanted to see regular results and consistent business growth, I would have to make marketing a priority and learn to find time for my writing. (No, the irony isn't lost on me...I'm a *writer* and still wasn't finding time for my own writing!)

Fortunately, there is a trick (or several, I should say) to finding time to write compelling marketing materials. Please check out the Feature Article below to find out exactly how you can make marketing a regular part of your business-building routine.

As always, please let me know if you have any questions or comments.

Hope you enjoy the article...and the rest of your week! ☺

Best,

Tammi Metzler
Chief Copywriter ~ The Write Associate
http://www.writeassociate.com
tammim@writeassociate.com
402.680.2311

<><><><><><><><><><><><><><><><><><><><>

2) Biz Booster of the Week

In the two years that I've been in business, I've picked up a *lot* of great business resources. There are some outstanding products, services, and software out there that can make an entrepreneur's life *so much* easier, but it can be hard to separate the junk from the life-changing, oh-so-worth-the-c0st goodies.

This week's Biz Booster is:

A pretty cool program called MarketMeTweet. This free download lets you promote your website from each and every tweet. You know how the bottom of each tweet lists a time and date stamp, followed by the method of delivery (i.e. from web, from TweetDeck, etc.)? Well, with MarketMeTweet, you can put whatever you want in the "from" space!

For example, mine says "from TheWriteAssociate" and includes a link back to my website (yep, you can add a link too!). Click here to see an example on my Twitter page: http://twitter.com/writeassociate.

The only downside is that you have to open the program to send tweets, and it doesn't let you see tweets from people you're following or @ responses, so you have to switch back and forth between Twitter and the MarketMeTweet program. Can be a bit cumbersome if you're in a hurry, but overall, it's a very impressive tool to potentially drive more traffic to your website. So, it's worth the minor inconvenience, in my book!

Click here to download the program at no charge: http://www.marketmetweet.com/tweetbrand-get-it-now.html

I think they do have an upgrade option that might offer more features, but I haven't looked into that yet. If you're using the upgrades or have any thoughts on this program, give me a shout;
I'd love to hear from you!

<><><><><><><><><><><><><><><><><><><><><><>

3) ** FEATURE ARTICLE **

Finding Time for Marketing When There's No Time to Write by Tammi Metzler

When it comes to marketing, consistency is key to great results. The question of the day is: How do you find time to write regular marketing messages, especially when you can barely have time for everything else on your already-overloaded plate? Following are a few tips and tricks that I've found very helpful in maintaining a regular marketing schedule:

- **Establish a marketing schedule.** If you don't already have a marketing schedule (or marketing plan, as it's otherwise known), putting one together can save you loads of time and stress. Trust me, I'm speaking from experience! I used to struggle to put out my marketing on a regular basis, and weeks would pass without a peep from me. I was just too busy with client work to worry about marketing! But I finally sat down and created a solid marketing plan, and it's been smooth sailing ever since. For example, you can plan to publish your email newsletter every Tuesday (or the last Thursday of the month, or whatever schedule works best for you, just as long as it's consistent), post to your blog every Wednesday, and write a press release on the first Monday of each quarter. That's just a sample of a marketing plan you might choose to create. For more on creating effective internet marketing plans, check out my recent teleseminar, "Get Clients With Less Effort: The Busy Entrepreneur's Step-by-Step Guide to a Client-Attracting Internet Marketing Plan" at www.writeassociate.com/products.

- **Treat marketing deadlines as seriously as you would client deadlines.** Now that you have a schedule in place, it's important to stick to it as closely as possible. Think of it this way: If you promised to complete a client project on Tuesday, you'd do whatever it took to get the job done on Tuesday, right? Try to treat your marketing with the same urgency and level of importance (because it is important...to the health and success of your business!).

- **Brainstorm ideas in advance.** I've learned that one of the top reasons for procrastination with writing and marketing is not knowing what to write about, so these tasks get put off. The fear of the unknown, you might say! Speaking from experience, this can be a tough hurdle to cross. To get past this, plan a brainstorming hour once a month. Sit down in a quiet place and jot down anything that you could potentially write about. Think about topics in your area of expertise, current trends, and frequently asked questions from clients. Don't censor yourself; just let the thoughts flow and get them down as quickly as you can! You can always weed through them later to pick the best topics. If you're still drawing a blank after a few minutes, start browsing blogs or articles from others within your industry (you can find popular blogs in any industry at Technorati.com). Of course, you would never steal their words...just use others' thoughts as inspiration for your own, unique marketing materials. Once you have a few good ideas, fill in a marketing calendar with the main subject of each blog post, article, newsletter, etc., that you plan to publish that month. If you have enough ideas, keep going into the next month, and the next, and so on. The more you plan in advance, the less time you'll need to spend trying to come up with good ideas, and the less likely you'll be to put off your marketing.

The bottom line is that if you want to grow your business, you have to make time for marketing and writing. And hey, once you get past the marketing procrastination trap, you just might find that marketing (and getting new clients as a result) is actually fun!

ABOUT THE AUTHOR: Client-attracting Web Copywriter Tammi Metzler of The Write Associate helps service professionals worldwide fight procrastination and create client-attracting web copy and marketing materials. Visit http://ClientAttractingWebCopy.com today to schedule a no-obligation phone chat where you can share your marketing struggles, seek help with brainstorming topic ideas for your marketing, and talk about potential marketing solutions to help your business succeed.

NOTE: You're welcome to re-use this article on your website or in your e-newsletter as long as it remains complete and unaltered, including the "About the Author" section at the end.

<><><><><><><><><><><><><><><><><><><><><><><>

4) Advertising section

Want to get more clients with your website?
Visit http://ClientAttractingWebCopy.com
and check out our brand new internet
marketing programs for service professionals
and home-based entrepreneurs!

 For information about affordable advertising
opportunities, please email us at
tammim@writeassociate.com and we'll be
happy to provide you with a no-obligation quote.

~^

5) About The Write Associate

The Write Associate helps service professionals
create compelling web copy that sells their services.
Working closely with clients, we help them discover

their target market and write copy that speaks directly to the needs of their potential clients, resulting in increased confidence and greater response rates. Providing quality work in a timely manner is our promise; our job is never complete until clients are thrilled with the results. Our affordability, professionalism, and sheer enthusiasm combine to create a copywriting experience that isn't soon forgotten by our clients or the people they serve. To schedule a get-acquainted phone chat that will help you discover whether our web copywriting and internet marketing services are right for your business, please visit www.writeassociate.com.

<><><><><><><><><><><><><><><><><><><><><><>

Your feedback is always welcome and appreciated! Please send your comments, questions, or concerns to tammim@writeassociate.com. We look forward to hearing from you!

"Copywriting to Get Clients" respects your privacy and *does not* give out or sell our subscribers' names and/or e-mail addresses...EVER!

<><><><><><><><><><><><><><><><><><><><><><>

You've received this e-zine because you've subscribed to it. To be removed from our list, please see the end of this e-mail.

Please feel free to pass along this issue to friends and associates -- just keep the entire message intact. Thanks!

And here's a template you can use for your own purposes:

{Newsletter name}
{Publisher name} (for small biz owners, this will likely be your name)
mailto:email address

<><><><><><><><><><><><><><><><><><><><><>

1) A note from {your first name}

Hi [fname],

Personal note introducing the feature article

{Salutation}

<><><><><><><><><><><><><><><><><><><><><>

2) ** FEATURE ARTICLE **

Headline
byline

Article body

© info

ABOUT THE AUTHOR:

NOTE: You're welcome to re-use this article on your website or in your
e-newsletter as long as it remains complete and unaltered, including the
"About the Author" section at the end.

<><><><><><><><><><><><><><><><><><><><><>

3) Advertising section

For information about affordable advertising
opportunities, please email us at
{your email address} and we'll be
happy to provide you with a no-obligation quote.

~∧

4) About {your company's name}

Bio, including link to your website for more information

<><><><><><><><><><><><><><><><><><><><><><><>

Your feedback is always welcome and appreciated!
Please send your comments, questions, or concerns to
{your email address}. We look forward to hearing
from you!

{Newsletter name} respects your privacy and
does not give out or sell our subscribers' names
and/or e-mail addresses...EVER!

<><><><><><><><><><><><><><><><><><><><><><><>

You've received this e-zine because you've subscribed to it.
To be removed from our list, please see the end of this e-mail.

All you really need for a great e-newsletter is a new
article and a brief introductory paragraph or two. As you
get more proficient, then you can add other sections,

such as the Biz Booster and Advertising sections that you see on my e-newsletter example. Don't overwhelm yourself with too much right off the bat, though; once you get comfortable with just sending your updated e-newsletter on a regular basis, then you can start adding other bells and whistles, such as a fancy HTML template that all the "gurus" out there use (unless you'd prefer to start with that – it's your choice).

Here's an example of what an HTML newsletter header looks like (taken from a recent issue of my e-newsletter):

March 9, 2010   Issue # 19

A Note From Tammi

Hi John,

Hope you're doing well! After an unbelievable response rate to the f.ree marketing evaluation offer that I sent out a few weeks back, I've talked to dozens of solo entrepreneurs about their marketing to figure out what's working and what is just wasting their time and money.

Case study: Format of a successful e-newsletter

My newsletter has been designed to do several things, but mostly its consistent format helps the reader to get familiar with who I am, what I offer and what to expect. I always start with an article designed to shift a common perspective or response to some usual small business scenario. This adds to my credibility. Then I insert a brief case study demonstrating varied needs and solutions, helping the reader to see their own situation in the story. I also use the newsletter to promote my upcoming events and make an offer.

Over the years, my newsletter has generated a variety of benefits: it's helped me to focus my marketing efforts by creating sub lists, given what links are opened by different people. It also has helped to fill my events. And, when I've asked readers to complete market research surveys, I get a good response rate because their experience with me tells them it's not a frivolous request. Also, whenever I've attended networking events, at least one person will approach me to tell me they read my newsletter and don't delete it when it shows up in their in box. I've gained 2 clients that I know of directly as a result of the newsletter, although it's used more as a means to get people into my pipeline and down into the product/service purchase opportunities.

 **Andrea Feinberg,** M.B.A., C.P.B.A., is President of Coaching Insight, LLC which identifies and leverages underused assets for small business clients. As a Wall Street executive, wholesale gift business owner, marketing consultant, and coach Andrea has 30 years experience helping clients articulate, achieve and exceed their goals, whether for business or personal lives. The key to her action-oriented business process is a simple yet powerful concept - *how* we respond to the realities and circumstances of our businesses has a fundamental impact on *what* those realities and circumstances are. Clients have included Standard & Poor's Corporation, Integ, Sandler Sales Institute, Cameron Advertising, The Marketing Resource Group, Provista Group, KMF Property Management, Certified Payroll, and others.

If you want to go with the more colorful HTML version – which I tend to prefer because readers get to see your smiling face, therefore increasing that know, like, and trust factor we keep talking about, you may need to hire a designer to help you – or take the time to tinker with it yourself if you have CSS and/or HTML knowledge.

If you don't know a good designer, see the Appendix at the end of this book for recommendations.

In a nutshell: Whether you choose a text template or HTML, just put *some* sort of template together and save it to your computer where you can easily access it each time you sit down to write the next issue. Once you have the set-up complete, you can just plug the new info in and send it off, shaving hours off your marketing time and just plain making your life a whole lot easier.

Chapter 9: Write Your E-newsletter Issues

Creating each issue of your e-newsletter doesn't have to be complicated. I've seen people doing many different things with their e-newsletters, including:

- Tip of the week/month – include an explanatory paragraph or two, and you're good to go!

- Video e-newsletters – if you're already doing video marketing, plug your videos into your e-newsletter (if possible – otherwise, describe the video and include a link where interested parties can view it online).

- Audio e-newsletters – same concept as above, but with podcast issues instead of videos.

- Blog recap – this is basically showcasing your blog posts for the month, giving a recap of each post and including links if readers want to learn more about each topic.

And then, of course, you have the widely popular written e-newsletters, which include at least one article (and in some cases, three or four – but I definitely think one is enough!) and maybe some other basic sections, like a recommendation area, advertising section, etc.

If you can write a 300-400 word article on your topic of expertise, you can publish an e-newsletter.

Outsource it!

If the thought of trying to come up with fresh content – or just the thought of writing, period – is competing with a root canal for top ranking on your "things I hate to do" list, you can always outsource your e-newsletter publishing to others.

Once you get in with a great ghostwriter, you can put the whole thing on autopilot, with your writer providing custom-written newsletter articles on a pre-determined schedule so that you just have to plug them into your newsletter template and press send. So easy! (If you'd like recommendations for newsletter writers, please see the Appendix.)

Do it yourself article template

Otherwise, if you'd rather write your own articles, check out the easy-to-follow article template on the following page.

Article title/Subject line: Your article title should pull double duty by being used as your e-newsletter subject line as well. The title is the most important part of your article, since an ineffective title/subject line means your article won't get read! I often leave this part for last, after I've written the article itself, so I can make sure the title really gets the right message across and fits in with what my article is about. Please refer to the title brainstorming suggestions beginning on page 43 – those tips will work for your article titles/e-newsletter subject lines as well.

Introduction: Write a paragraph explaining the main topic of your article in a way that will grab the reader's attention and convince them to read more. You don't have to get bland here, either – even in non-fiction articles, you can unleash your creativity. Example: "The time was 5:00 p.m., and Karen was dreading yet another frustrating drive home through rush-hour traffic. If only she knew the secrets of building a profitable home-based business that I'm going to share with you today…"

Body: After the introduction paragraph, you'll get into the "meat" of your article, sharing specific tips and techniques on your subject matter. If the topic can be broken into several parts, use subheadings to make it easy for readers to scan the article and find exactly what they want to read. In the example above, the main subject is building a profitable home-based business, and the subheadings might be Choosing the Right Business Model, Deciding What to Sell, and Setting Up Your Home Office.

Don't be afraid to use lists and bullet points to break up the text and further feed into readers' natural tendency to scan.

Conclusion: In the last paragraph, briefly restate the main points from your article and give readers a specific action to take. It may look something like this:

"In conclusion, if you want to build a profitable business from home, you'll need to choose the right business model, decide what to sell, and set up your home office. Get started today by creating a timeframe for completing each step, and you'll soon be on your way to a profitable home business!"

Author Resource Box: Your author resource box should appear at the bottom of each article, and you should use this prime space to drive traffic back to your website for a specific reason. For example, if you're hosting an upcoming teleseminar that will give more information on the subject in your article, your author resource box would give a brief, one-line description of who you are and who you help, and then you would use the rest of the space (another sentence or two, tops) to tell people about the teleseminar and how they can sign up.

Here's an example of the resource box I often use (sometimes I switch it up a bit, depending on the content of my article and the action I want readers to take):

Client-Attracting Website Copywriter Tammi Metzler of The Write Associate is on a mission to help self-employed service professionals worldwide create thriving

newsletter communities full of hot prospects. Get her
FREE report, "3 Insider Secrets to Whipping Up Website
Copy That Makes You Money!" by visiting
www.ClientAttractingWebCopy.com.

Before we go any further, let's dive a little deeper into
the subject of the all-important author resource box.

The Author Resource box

The "job" of an author resource box is to attract interest
from potential clients who are already interested in your
topic so that they can come back to your website and
either find their way into your marketing funnel or, for
those already on your newsletter list, to buy your
products and services. This goal is the whole point of
article marketing: establish your expertise first, and then
drive interested readers back to your website to sign up
for your e-newsletter or contact you for more
information. Otherwise, if readers don't take further
action to get into your marketing funnel, you're just
wasting time and effort.

Okay, back to the specifics of the author resource box.
Your author resource box should appear at the bottom of
each article you write, and you should use this prime
space to drive traffic back to your website for a specific
reason. For example, if you have a free report that gives
more information on the subject in your article, your
author resource box would give a brief, one-line
description of who you are and who you help, and then

you would use the rest of the space (another sentence or two, tops) to tell people about the free report and how to sign up.

When it comes to the Author Resource box in articles that you publish in your email newsletter, you don't want to direct people to download your free report, of course; they're already on your newsletter list, so you don't need to get them to give you their contact information in exchange for a free gift. In this case, you'll want to use the Author Resource box to promote a paid product or service, such as an upcoming program that relates to the topic within the article, perhaps.

Let's take a closer look at my author resource box example noted on the previous page:

Client-Attracting Website Copywriter Tammi Metzler of The Write Associate is on a mission to help self-employed service professionals worldwide create thriving newsletter communities full of hot prospects. Get her FREE report, "3 Insider Secrets to Whipping Up Website Copy That Makes You Money!" by visiting www.ClientAttractingWebCopy.com.

The yellow highlighted portion is the sentence about who I am, whom I help, and what I do for them, and then the pink highlighted section is the promo for the free report they can request to learn more about the topic at hand.

All too often, service professionals try to use their author resource box to sell their services, but really this space would be better used to get interested prospects into your marketing funnel by offering them a free gift. From there, you can begin building a relationship with them and ease them into purchasing your products and services once they know, like, and trust you.

Use attention-grabbing words

One last tip: Don't forget to use attention-grabbing words in your author resource box, like:

- Affordable

- Crucial

- Bottom line

- Breakthrough

- Easy

- Effective

- Free

- Groundbreaking

- High yield

- Innovative

- Limited time

- New

- Novel

- Opportunities

- Results oriented

- Rewards

- Revolutionary

(Note: These attention-grabbing words are also good for article titles and email newsletter subject lines.)

What will your author resource box say? Start with a brief sentence about who you are, whom you help, and what you can do for them:

_____

_____

_____

And then end with a sentence inviting them to download your free giveaway (don't forget to tell them how/where!):

_____

_____

_____

Now, put it together here:

_____

_____

_____

_____

_____

_____

Now that you're armed with your Author Resource box and your easy article template, you've got everything you need to write a great e-newsletter.

One last tip before we move on to building your newsletter list: after you write your article, and paste in your author resource box, be sure to conclude with the following statement, placed directly underneath your author resource box:

NOTE: You're welcome to re-use this article on your website or in your e-newsletter as long as it remains complete and unaltered, including the "About the Author" section at the end.

Case study: The key to a great newsletter

A newsletter is not just a collection of articles. The message given must reflect your core message, support your ongoing theme or focus and **be exquisitely crafted**.

 For more than 20 years, DeBorah Beatty has been a coach and trainer helping startup, work-at-home, freelance, and mom-and-pop businesses save time and money by reducing the amount of back office time and increasing productivity while decreasing production time, getting you back to the business of your business and not the tedium of paperwork and humdrum day-to-day activities. She's been involved with direct sales, online sales, telemarketing sales, home-based businesses, traveling craftsperson sales at outside festivals (which she still does as an exhibiting artist) and always has found ways to do the same things as the big companies but on a much smaller budget and little or no staff.

Brainstorming e-newsletter topics

Okay, so now that you know what goes in your e-newsletter, how do you figure out what to fill it with?

Ask your target what they want to know

Get on Twitter, Facebook, or online networking forums you belong to and ask people what questions they'd like answered (that apply to your area of expertise, of course). You can also ask your email list, if you have one. For the most part, if you ask for suggestions and make it clear that you're trying to provide them with information that they're looking for, they will take the time to answer!

Use case studies

Ask your current clients if you can turn your work with them (on a specific project, maybe) into a case study that proves your expertise; you can also get inspiration from your social networking groups by asking people for specific instances of things they've struggled with recently, in terms of a very specific topic. For example, if you help people organize their workspaces, ask people if there was a time recently when they wasted a lot of time or got frustrated because they couldn't find a document they were looking for. In an article or blog post, you can talk about their situation (with their permission, of course) and how you would suggest they make changes for better results.

Research other popular article titles

Now, I would never suggest that you copy other article titles, but you can find out what people are searching for and use that info to create your own article on a similar topic. One idea is to see what people are reading on EzineArticles, one of the top article directories out there. To do that, go to Google and type in a keyword that you're interested in writing about.

Enter a space and then add the following code:

site:ezinearticles.com "This article has been viewed 2000..199999" "Article Submitted On: * *, 2010"

You'll see articles that have been looked at more than 2000 times at EzineArticles, which can help you find hot topics people are looking for. You can change the "2000" in the code to alter the minimum amount of views returned, and you can also change the year from 2010 to get the returns for articles published in previous years. This tool can help you pick popular titles so you can focus on what people are reading most on EzineArticles.

Action step: Be sure to record all of the potential article topics (whether you think you'll use them now or not – they still might come in handy when your idea well is dry a few months down the road) in one easy-to-find spot. Where you put them is up to you; you can dedicate one notebook (that you keep nearby at all times) to topic ideas or have a Word doc on your computer that holds all of your topic ideas. Every month or two, grab the top few topics and put them into an editorial calendar to schedule out your marketing for the month.

Chapter 10: Build Your Newsletter List

Once you have your e-newsletter in place and ready to begin publishing to the masses, it's time to start building your newsletter list! There are several ways you can go about building your mailing list, so let's dive in to cover a few of them, shall we?

Let your e-newsletter articles serve double duty

If you've written an article for your e-newsletter, the best way to leverage your time is to publish that same article to your website (such as in an Article Library section like I have at http://writeassociate.com/article-library/). Then take the article and submit it to various article directories, which are essentially websites that host articles for people searching for information.

Here are some of the top article directories in terms of traffic:

- Ezinearticles.com
- Articlesbase.com
- Suite101.com (but you have to be approved as a writer for this one)
- Goarticles.com
- Helium.com

Submit your e-newsletter to directories

Similar to article directories, there are more and more e-zine/e-newsletter directories popping up online where you can submit your e-newsletter and free giveaway in an effort to get new subscribers. Some of these directories get a large amount of traffic, making them a great way to get your e-newsletter in front of new prospects at no cost to you (other than your time, of course).

Here are a few free options:

http://new-list.com/submit/

http://bestezines.com/submit/

http://zinos.com/cool/zinos/submitzine.html

http://www.listchannel.com/cgi-bin/dir/add.cgi

Display your free giveaway prominently on every page of your website

I've had clients complain about not having enough subscribers to their newsletters, and then when I look at their websites, I can't even find their sign-up form. Sometimes it's buried at the bottom of their pages, and sometimes it's just on the home page – which is often a well-trafficked page, but you'll still have some visitors coming into other pages, and you want to have a way to capture their contact information as well. If you click through some of the pages on my website (www.writeassociate.com), you'll see that my sign-up form appears on the landing page and also on the right sidebar of every single page. The form is built into the template of my website, so any time I add a page to my website, the header and sidebar automatically appear on that page. If you don't know how to edit CSS/HTML to create your own website templates, you will save a LOT of time, money, and headaches if you hire a designer to take care of the whole thing for you. For affordable web design recommendations, please see the Appendix.

Utilize your email signature line

You probably send dozens, if not hundreds, of emails each day, right? Whether you're chatting with friends, colleagues, or potential clients, including promotions in your email signature line is a non-intrusive way to get new subscribers without much effort on your part. In fact, once you set up the initial signature line, there's no extra effort – the promotion will automatically show up in every email you write. Many email programs, such as Outlook, or even web-based programs like Gmail, have an option to create a signature line. If you use Firefox as your internet browser, there's a free add-on called Wisestamp that allows you to create fancy signature lines such as the following:

Best,

Tammi Metzler
Client-Attracting Web Copy Specialist
Ph: 402.680.2311
tammim@writeassociate.com
www.writeassociate.com
For FREE Client-Attracting Web Copy tips, visit http://ClientAttractingWebCopy.com

Let's connect:

Chat ☺Skype: writeassociate

Contact Me 🔲🔲

--- @ WiseStamp Signature. Get it now

Wisestamp is great because it automatically inserts your signature line into any of your web-based email programs, so whether you're using Gmail, Yahoo, Hotmail, etc., all you have to do is click Compose to start a new email, and your signature line will show up.

Wisestamp also plugs in the icons for social networking sites such as Twitter, Facebook, and LinkedIn – the three I have in my email signature line – and if you click any of them, it will take readers directly to your profile page so they can connect with you there. (And no, I'm not affiliated with Wisestamp in any way...I'm just a big fan!)

Notice how, in my signature line, the invitation to download my free report is bolded to help it stand out; honestly, if people notice anything in my signature line, I want it to be that invitation!

The beauty of using signature lines is that in addition to the people you're emailing directly, anyone who sees a forward of that email will see your signature line as well – so as I mentioned previously, even if you're using your email for personal things, you just never know when a friend of a friend might be your ideal client – and your next subscriber.

To write your own signature line, all you really need is your contact information and a one-line teaser, like "Free Report: Discover 10 Hidden Techniques to Shed Those Last 10 Pounds - For Good!" Follow it with a link to your free report's opt-in page, and proceed to send emails as usual. Free, instant advertising to everyone you come in contact with!

Take advantage of your offline marketing efforts

Add the same teaser as the above (or a slightly different one, if you want to shake things up a bit) to your business cards, brochures, fliers, etc. Alternatively, if you plan to change your free giveaway anytime soon, you might want to stick with something a little more generic. (I change mine about every three months or so, but this definitely isn't required; a good free giveaway could be used for years. I just get tired of mine after a while and get the itch to try something new!) As an example, you could write something like, "FREE Client-attracting tips at http://WriteAssociate.com" (using your own info, of course). Since all of my articles, reports, and other website content revolve around getting clients, this statement will always work, even if I change my free giveaway on a whim.

The bottom line is that making this simple tweak to your offline marketing materials can be an enticing, non-intrusive way to get interested prospects from the offline world to request your free giveaway – and get into your marketing funnel.

Find a few good JV partners

Other professionals who serve the same target market as you can potentially offer ideal joint venture (JV) partnerships. These JV projects can be as simple as:

- Running guest articles in each others' newsletters – just don't forget to include a compelling About the Author section that invites people to visit your website and sign up for your e-newsletter

- Reviewing and recommending each others' free giveaways and/or e-newsletters within your e-newsletter issues

- Swapping advertising space within each others' e-newsletters

Be sure to choose a JV partner who targets the same market as you but isn't directly competing with you. Here are a few examples of strong JV partnerships:

- A business coach who works with home-based entrepreneurs might partner with a virtual assistant who serves the same market. This match would be good because they aren't offering the same services and, therefore, wouldn't be taking business away from each other.

- A nutritionist and a personal trainer could potentially form multiple JV partnerships because of their complementary services. They could form a joint weight-loss program, co-author a health & fitness book, or co-host a paid teleseminar or webinar about a hot topic in weight loss. The possibilities are virtually endless!

- A copywriter and a website designer can work together to create complete websites for clients, offering both design and copy services (such as I did with website designer Darlene Victoria

Gonzalez on our JV project, Webcentric Web Design – you can see how we structured our JV partnership by visiting www.WebcentricWebDesign.com).

I love JV partnerships because you can essentially double your marketing efforts without doubling your workload. If you already have a somewhat established client base (or Twitter following, etc.) and you choose another professional who also has a similarly established client base, you can broadcast each other's messages to your own community – and each of you will benefit from increased exposure and potential new clients. I love win-win situations, and in my opinion, JV partnerships are the epitome of an opportunity where everybody wins – the client or prospect (who gets more information on a topic that they're already interested in), yourself, and your JV partner.

Wrapping it up

While growing a profitable newsletter list doesn't typically happen overnight, you can take the steps mentioned in this chapter to put yourself well on your way to your own thriving community of eager-to-buy clients.

Final Word From The Author

A strong marketing funnel can, quite literally, make or break your business. I've heard horror stories of companies who had at one point experienced massive success thanks to high search engine placements – yet once Google changed its search engine optimization algorithm (as Google tends to do on a whim), they lost first page rankings in Google and took such a hit that they had to shut down shop. Yikes!

The same can be true with other advertising mediums as well; maybe you've been running a small, yet effective, ad in a local magazine geared toward your target market for years, and because of an inexperienced new editor or a change in management, the readership starts to dwindle and you're left scrambling for customers.

It can really happen to any business at any time, but of course, small business owners are much more susceptible to these dangers. If you have a strong community of loyal customers who are eager to hear from you month after month and who truly value your products and services, however, you'll never want for potential customers (or new business).

It has to be a two-way street, however; if you want your community to value you, you should value your community as well. You should be surveying them regularly to make sure you're meeting their needs, and your products and services should be of the highest possible quality. Otherwise, they'll look elsewhere for their weight loss guidance, or copywriting assistance, or whatever it is you happen to offer.

I hope you've found this book useful on your quest for business success. If you should have any questions or concerns, please don't hesitate to contact my team at support@writeassociate.com.

To your success,

Tammi Metzler

About the Author

Client-attracting website copywriter
Tammi Metzler has helped countless
service professionals worldwide
create client-attracting web copy and
marketing materials. Visit
http://ClientAttractingWebCopy.com
to snag a free copy of her latest client-
attracting tips report, register for free
monthly teleseminars on creating
client-attracting websites and email
newsletters, or set up a get-

acquainted phone call to share your marketing struggles, ask
internet marketing questions that you're dying to get
answered, and talk about potential solutions.

FREE Gifts!

Check out these free gifts available on Tammi's website:

Free report: "3 Insider Secrets to Whipping Up Website Copy That Makes You Money!"

All too many small business owners throw up a website and then spend all of their time trying to drive traffic to their new site...only to watch in frustration as their visitors don't DO anything. If you want to build a website that brings a steady stream of paying clients and hot prospects into your service business, then you won't want to miss this powerful report.

Free download: "Autoresponder Messages That SELL Your Products and Services!"

Now that you have the basics for publishing a profitable newsletter, you can get instant access to a series of emails that can be sent out to your new subscribers – and bring in sales of your products and services, time and time again – from one initial effort. Just plug your information into these templates, copy and paste them into your email autoresponder, and wait for the sales to come rolling in!

Free business analysis: *Tap Into the Potential of Explosive Success in Your Business*

Claim one of 8 no-charge marketing consultations each month, during which you will get direct access to Tammi Metzler for a no-holds-barred, 15-minute phone conversation to identify the roadblocks you're facing and determine the solutions that are just right for your situation.

To grab these gifts (plus check for new ones!), please visit http://writeassociate.com/free-gifts/.

Appendix

Below are some of the valuable resources that can help you create your own profitable newsletters.

Email Autoresponders
iContact
http://www.thewriteassociate.icontact.com

Email Newsletter Management
Tammi Metzler ~ The Write Associate
Whether you hate to write, don't know how to monetize your newsletter, or just don't have time to stay up on your email newsletters, she can help you publish effective email newsletters. Just visit the link below and scroll down to "Email newsletter management" to learn more!
http://writeassociate.com/services/

Email Signature Software
Wisestamp
http://www.wisestamp.com/

Email Newsletter HTML Templates
Darlene Victoria Gonzalez ~ Webcentric Web Design
A well-designed HTML template for your email newsletter can instantly create a polished, professional image for your newsletter. (Hint: it can also skyrocket your credibility and expert status.) Just visit the link below, scroll down to "Email newsletter set-up," and select "Create HTML newsletter."
http://writeassociate.com/services/

Internet Marketing Education

The Beginner's Guide to Internet Marketing: How to Get Clients With Less Effort

Now that you know how to use email newsletters effectively, discover how to choose among the most popular forms internet marketing to find the methods that will work best for you – and begin driving droves of traffic to your website.

http://writeassociate.com/products

Marketing Consulting

Tammi Metzler ~ The Write Associate

Her in-depth Strategy Sessions are designed for entrepreneurs who are frustrated by their underperforming (or non-performing!) marketing and want to strategize how to get more clients and make money from their efforts. Whether you're just starting out or have been online for 5 years, she can guarantee that you'll pick up a few pointers to dramatically increase your results – or get your money back!

http://www.WriteAssociate.com/home

Opt-in Page Creation

Tammi Metzler & Darlene Victoria Gonzalez ~ Webcentric Web Design

If you're serious about growing your newsletter list, this dynamic duo can provide you with a customized opt-in page, complete with a branded web design template and compelling copy that will convince visitors to subscribe now! Just visit the link below and take a look at the "Squeeze/sales page creation" option.

http://writeassociate.com/services/

Print Newsletter Direct Mail Services
MailFinch
https://www.mailfinch.com/

Survey Tools
JotForm
http://www.jotform.com/

Survey Monkey
http://www.surveymonkey.com

Bonus Articles

The following articles were taken from my email newsletter, Copywriting to Get Clients. This bi-weekly publication has a $97 annual value, but you can get a free subscription by visiting http://writeassociate.com/free-gifts.

If you have any questions, don't hesitate to contact us at support@writeassociate.com. Happy reading!

How to Write Compelling Article Titles that Get Your Articles Read
by Tammi Metzler

All too often, people spend the majority of their time researching and writing their articles and then end up throwing together an article title as an afterthought. While it's okay (and recommended, even) to create your title after writing the article, be sure to place careful consideration on the article title you're using. You want to choose an article title that convinces people to read your article; after all, even the best article in the world will gather dust if the article title isn't compelling enough people to read your message.

Following are a few types of article titles that are more likely to attract interest and compel readers to see what you have to say.

Compelling Article Title Type: The question

The human brain is hardwired to seek answers to questions, especially if it's a topic that even vaguely interests us. Think about the last time you were standing in line at the grocery store and glanced over at the magazine racks. Seeing a question in an article title that piqued your interest, you picked up the magazine and flipped to the article. After reading through the main points, you might have decided that the article was interesting or useful enough to buy the magazine so you could take it home and take a closer look at the article. And the article title just served its purpose: to sell a copy of the magazine.

When you're writing articles, it's going to be a bit different because you probably aren't trying to sell magazines, but the basic premise is the same: if you can get people to click through to your article, you are one step closer to gaining credibility as an expert in your field and, depending on the Author Resource box you use, you might even get a few new clients who click through to your website to contact you.

Some examples of intriguing questions might be:

"Is your doctor lying about your healthcare options?"

"Is your child at risk for cancer?"

"Is your business at risk for financial failure?"

Even if you think that your doctor, child, or business are fine, those questions could pose a nagging doubt that eats at you until you just have to glance through the article to make sure you're not missing something important.

Compelling Article Title Type: The List

The List article title is similar to the Question article title in that both are designed to pique your interest, but, as you might guess, the List article title is structured as a list of top tips or techniques. You still want to use "hot" words that are going to grab attention, like "free," "secret," etc.

Some examples might be:

"5 Ways to Keep Your Job in Today's Layoff-Friendly Economy"

"10 Signs That Your Marriage is in Trouble"

"3 Things You Should Know Before Serving Your Family's Next Meal"

All of the article titles above indicate to readers that there are things they don't know that could potentially be sabotaging their jobs, marriage, and family's health, respectively. These article titles promise to give answers (and they should, or they'd be misleading, and you'll actually lose credibility), and if readers like the info you have to offer, they'll be more likely to check out your other articles or visit your website to learn more about you.

Compelling Article Title Type: The How-to

How-to article titles tell readers that you're going to show them exactly how to do something, in a step-by-step manner. These are great for the many do-it-yourselfers out there who are looking for ways to solve their problems, right now.

Examples are:
"How to Double Your Income This Year"

"How to Get More Done in Less Time"

"How to Publish an E-zine that Gets You More Clients"

One caveat: be sure to only use a how-to article title if your article really does walk readers through the process of doing what you say you're going to teach them. If you say you're going to show people how to get more done, as in the second example, your article shouldn't talk entirely about why you should want to get more done in less time and conclude with a link back to your website, which offers services to help people organize their offices.

People will just be frustrated and maybe a bit ticked off at your deception, and they definitely won't be contacting you to work together. So be sure to actually give them a few tips to get more things done. You don't have to give away everything you know, but you do have to give some useful information. You may think that giving away information will keep people from hiring you, but in showing people firsthand that you're great at what you do, they'll be more likely to want to learn more about how you might be able to help them.

To avoid wasting your article marketing efforts, be sure to take the time to craft an article title that gets your article read. Because the more people who are out there reading your articles, the greater your chances of establishing yourself as an expert in your field and gaining the trust of potential clients, who will then be more likely to buy your products and services.

(c) 2009 The Write Associate

ABOUT THE AUTHOR: Client-attracting Web Copywriter Tammi Metzler of The Write Associate is on a mission to help service professionals worldwide create client-attracting web copy and marketing materials. Visit http://ClientAttractingWebCopy.com today to schedule a free website evaluation and see if your website is doing what it should to attract more clients for your service business!

NOTE: You're welcome to re-use this article on your website or in your e-newsletter as long as it remains complete and unaltered, including the "About the Author" section at the end.

Bonus Article #2

The 5 Most Powerful Words in Marketing
by Tammi Metzler

There are five unbelievably powerful words that you must consider before you even sit down to write your website copy and email newsletters.

These five powerful words are: What's In It For Me.

You may have heard of this referred to as the acronym: WIIFM. It may sound harsh, but visitors to your website simply don't care about what *you* do; they care about how what you do affects *them*.

Initially, at least, they only care about how you can help them get the results they seek, how you can help them solve their deepest and most painful problems. Then, once they've subconsciously made the decision to work with you, they may go digging around your website to learn more about you, your experience, your qualifications, what you've done for other clients, etc.

But mostly they want to know how your products and services will change their lives. If that business development course you're offering next month will share tricks to increase their productivity, marketing techniques to double their income, tips on hiring staff so the business owners can take more time off, etc., be sure to address those benefits. You're not just offering to help people grow their business...you're helping people improve their overall quality of life. But your website visitors won't know that unless you tell them...so be sure to tell them exactly what they will gain from buying your products and services.

Here are a few questions you can ask yourself to hone in on reasons that will hit home with your website visitors (and prospective clients):

1. What are some of the problems that your clients experienced before working with you? What are some of the solutions that you provided to them?
2. What are some of the "hot" issues that your target market is dying to solve?
3. What do potential clients stand to gain by buying your products and services?

Putting it all together

Now that you have an idea of the message you should convey in your website copy and email newsletters, it's time to input that information into your sales copy. Just make a point to speak directly to your potential clients and their needs, and you'll be well on your way to a client-attracting web presence!

To discover how to put all of the pieces together to create a website that attracts clients, visit http://writeassociate.com/upcoming-teleseminars/ to grab a copy of my F-REE teleseminar, "**The 5 Must-Have Elements of a Website That Will Instantly Establish Your Credibility, Form a Connection With Your Prospective Clients, and Get Your Website Visitors to Take Action!**"

(c) 2009 The Write Associate

ABOUT THE AUTHOR: Tammi Metzler is a Copywriter and Marketing Consultant who helps struggling entrepreneurs earn more money and skyrocket their business growth through the creation of effective marketing materials. Check out her free reports, articles, and other marketing resources by visiting www.WriteAssociate.com.

NOTE: You're welcome to re-use this article on your website or in your e-newsletter as long as it remains complete and unaltered, including the "About the Author" section at the end.

www.ingramcontent.com/pod-product-compliance
Lightning Source LLC
Chambersburg PA
CBHW051545170526
45165CB00002B/895